WHAT I LOVE ABOUT

GRANDPA

WRITTEN BY

_____

ADDITIONAL FREE RESOURCES

Visit:
www.rocketstudiobooks.com/love

Get:
- Ideas & inspiration to make your book pop!
- A page of all the questions to draft your answers

JOIN US ON INSTAGRAM
@LotusLovePress

LOTUS LOVE PRESS

01

I LOVE IT WHEN WE

_____

02

THANK YOU FOR TEACHING ME

_____

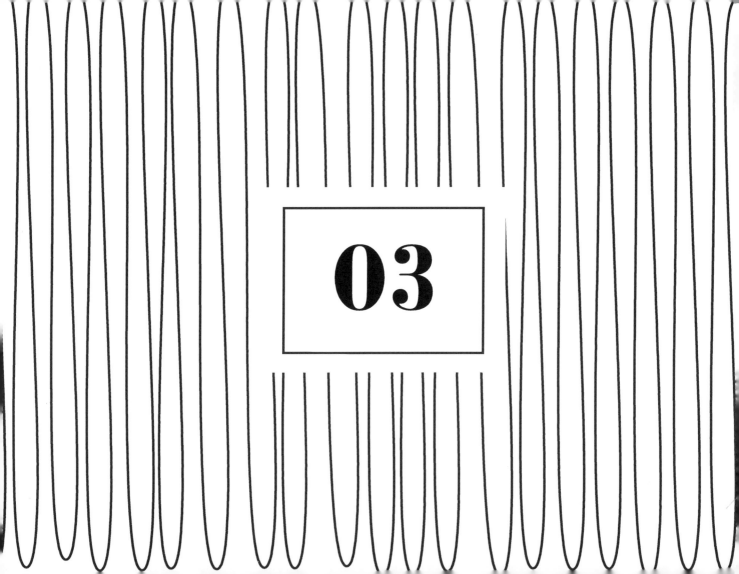

03

I KNOW YOU LOVE ME BECAUSE

_____

04

I LOVE HOW YOU ALWAYS

_____

THANK YOU FOR

_____

06

THE FUNNIEST THING ABOUT YOU IS

_____

YOU ARE REALLY GOOD AT

_____

I LOVE IT WHEN YOU SAY

_____

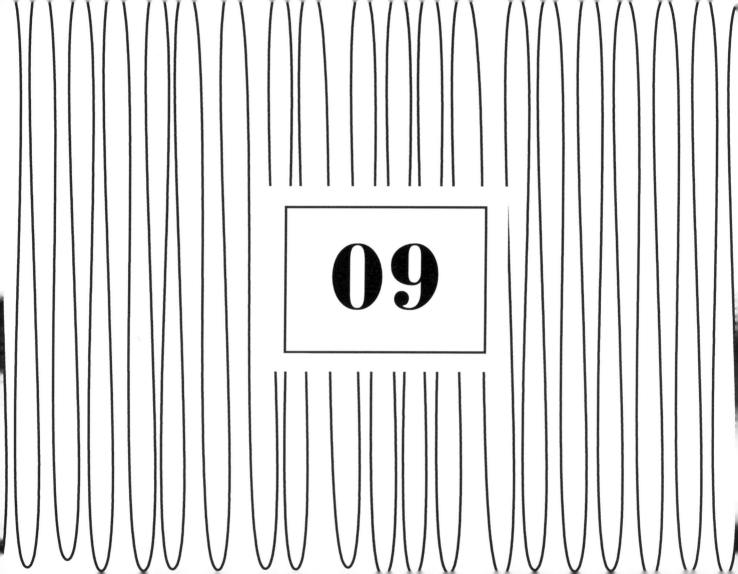

IF YOU WERE AN ANIMAL, YOU'D BE

_____

10

YOU MAKE ME LAUGH WHEN

_____

I'M GLAD WE

THE BEST THING ABOUT YOU IS

_____

13

YOU ARE BETTER THAN A

_____

YOU TAUGHT ME HOW TO

_____

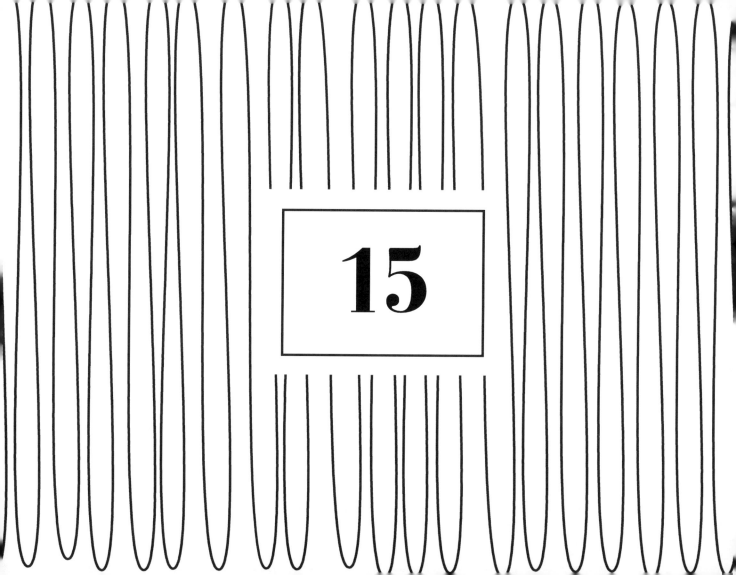

15

I LOVE HOW YOU NEVER GET TIRED OF

_____

16

I LOVE IT WHEN WE PLAY

_____

IF YOU WERE A DESSERT YOU'D BE

_____

WHEN YOU LOOK AT ME I FEEL

_____

19

MY FAVORITE THING WE'VE DONE WAS

_____

I LOVE TO WATCH YOU

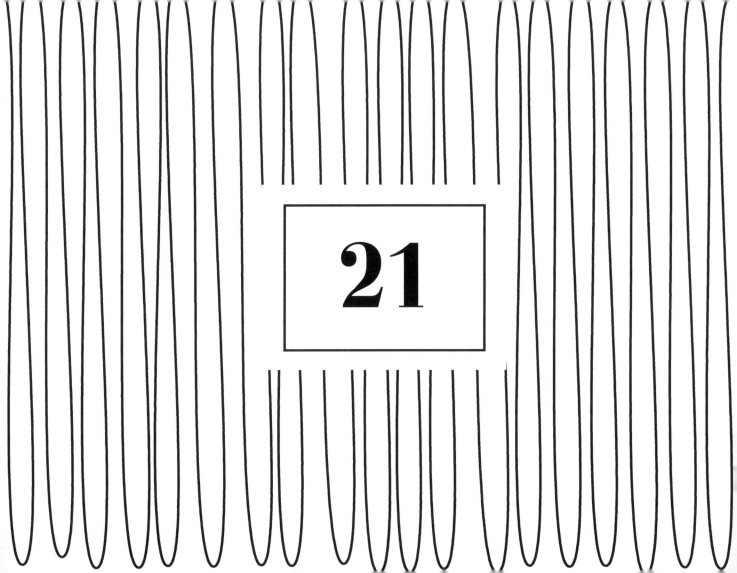

21

YOU MAKE ME WANT TO BE BETTER AT

_____

22

YOU MAKE THE BEST

ONE WORD TO DESCRIBE YOU IS

_____

24

IF YOU WERE A COLOR YOU'D BE

_____

25

I LOVE THAT YOU'RE MY GRANDPA BECAUSE

_____

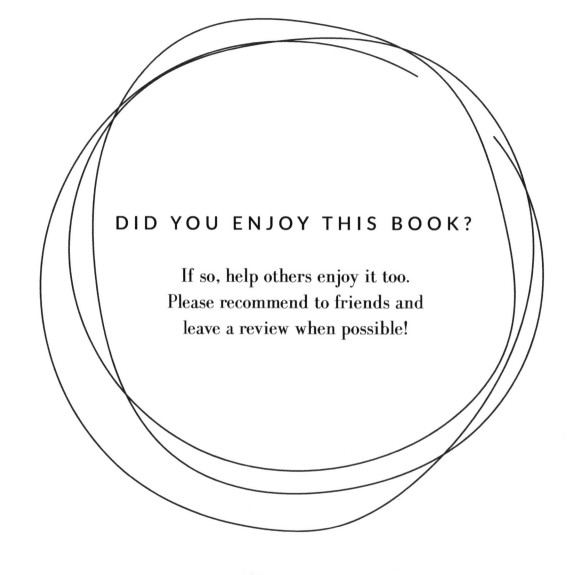

DID YOU ENJOY THIS BOOK?

If so, help others enjoy it too.
Please recommend to friends and
leave a review when possible!

THERE'S A BOOK FOR EVERYONE YOU LOVE!

Grandparents
Grandma
Nan
Nana
Nanna
Granny
Grammy
Gigi
Nonna
Mimi
Oma
Abuela
Grandad
Grandpa
Pa
Pop
Papa
Opa
Nonno

Parents
Mom
My Mommy
My Stepmom
Mum
My Mummy
My Stepmum
Dad
My Daddy
My Stepdad
My Wife
My Husband
My Boyfriend
My Girlfriend
My Partner
My Sister
My Brother
Things I Love about You

My Daughter
My Son
My Step Daughter
My Step Son
My Granddaughter
My Grandson
My Aunt
My Auntie
My Aunty
My Uncle
My Nephew
My Niece

SCAN ME

FIND US ON AMAZON

LOTUS LOVE PRESS

Made in the USA
Las Vegas, NV
11 December 2022